by **Lesléa Newman** Illustrated by **Susan G**

HERE IS THE WORLD

A YEAR OF JEWISH HOLIDAYS

Abrams Books for Young Readers, New York

The author offers special thanks to Rabbi Justin David, Rachel Kamin, and Mary Newman Vazquez for their assistance in creating this book.

The illustrations in this book were made with charcoal on paper and digital collage.

Library of Congress Cataloging-in-Publication Data

Newman, Lesléa.
Here is the world: a year of Jewish holidays / by Lesléa Newman ; Illustrated by Susan Gal.
pages cm
ISBN 978-1-4197-1185-5
1. Fasts and feasts—Judaism—Juvenile literature. 2. Jewish crafts—Juvenile literature. 3. Jewish cooking—Juvenile literature. I. Gal, Susan. II. Title.
BM690.N49 2014
296.4'3—dc23
2013029463

ISBN for this edition: 978-1-4197-1429-0

Text copyright © 2014 Lesléa Newman
Illustrations copyright © 2014 Susan Gal
Book design by Chad W. Beckerman

Printed and bound in China
10 9 8 7 6 5 4 3 2 1

101428K1

ABRAMS
THE ART OF BOOKS SINCE 1949

115 West 18th Street
New York, NY 10011
www.abramsbooks.com

For my mother, Florence Newman.
May her memory be a blessing.
&
Andrea Ayvazian,
sister in spirit.
—L.N.

For the Boyder family, especially Anne,
with gratitude and friendship.
—S.G.

Here are your parents, with arms open wide.
Here are your siblings, to stand by your side.

Here is the rabbi, with blessings to share.
Here is a wish and a hope and a prayer.

NAMING CEREMONY

SHABBAT

Here are two candles, with flames burning bright.
Here is the challah we eat Friday night.

Here is a yarmulke, here is a shawl.
Here is the synagogue, open to all.

Here are some clouds and a cool autumn breeze.

Here are the leaves, falling down from the trees.

Here is the shofar, its sound pure and sweet.
Here are some apples and honey to eat.

ROSH HASHANAH

Here is your family, all dressed in white.

YOM KIPPUR

Here is the Break-Fast to eat with delight.

Here is the sukkah, its roof made of twigs.
Here are some grapes, pomegranates, and figs.

SUKKOT

Here is the Torah, more precious than gold.
Here are the songs and the stories of old.

SIMCHAT TORAH

Here is the snow of a fierce winter storm.
Here we are snuggled in, cozy and warm.

Here's a menorah, with candles to light.
Here are some latkes. Come take the first bite!

CHANUKAH

TU B'SHEVAT

Here's a parade—come and march with the crowd!
Here is a grogger to shake nice and loud.

Here are the flowers that bloom in the spring.
Here are the birds that have come back to sing.

Here's a Haggadah to put at each chair.
Here is the matzah that's baked with such care.

PASSOVER

SHAVUOT

Here is a harvest of ripe golden wheat.
Here are some blintzes and milk for a treat.

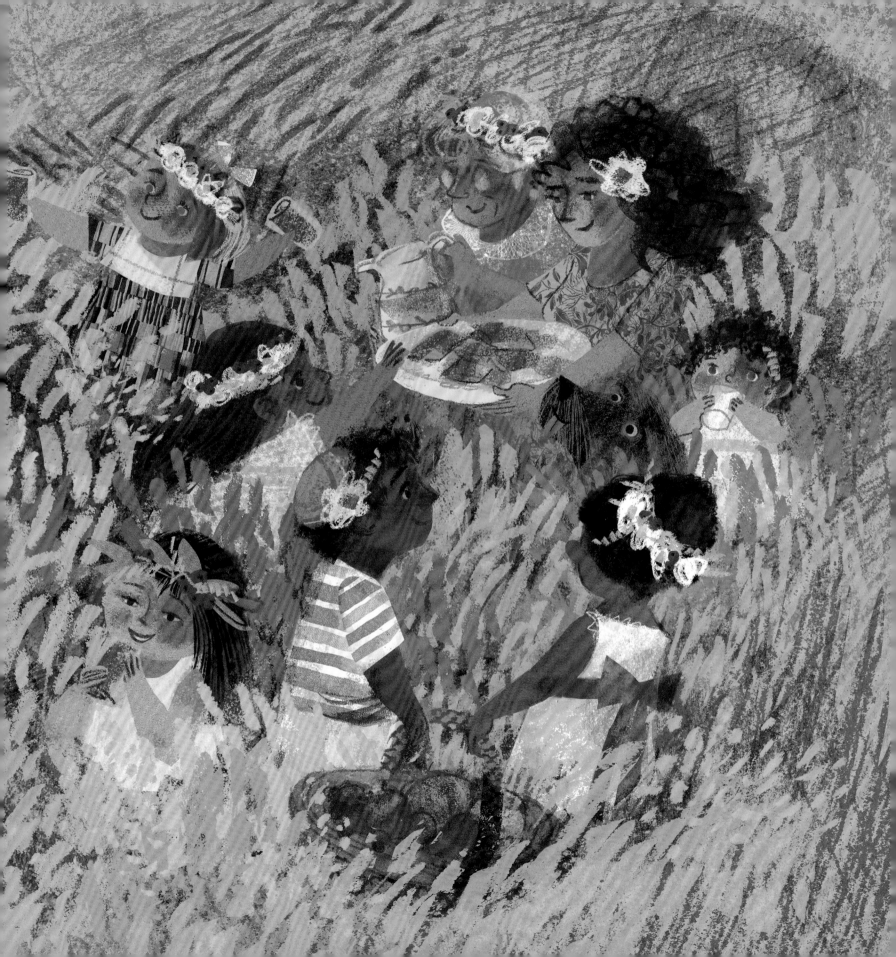

Here is a summer day, sunny and hot.
Here is a picnic to share on Shabbat.

SHABBAT

Here is the sun, beaming down from on high.
Here are the stars and the moon in the sky.

Here is the world, ever-changing and new,
Spinning with joy at the wonder of you!

JEWISH CUSTOMS AND HOLIDAYS

NAMING CEREMONY: The first Shabbat (Sabbath) after a baby girl is born is an exciting day! For many families, it's the day the new baby's naming ceremony, or *Simchat Bat*, takes place. Although there are no set rules as to when or where a Simchat Bat should be held, many parents take their daughter to the synagogue so that everyone can celebrate her birth and welcome her into the community. The baby's name is announced with joy, and special prayers for her are said. It is a time of great celebration! When a baby boy is born, it is traditional for his name to be announced at a ceremony called a *brit milah*, or *bris*, which takes place on the eighth day of the baby's life.

SHABBAT is the Hebrew word for "Sabbath," and it's a holiday celebrated every week of the year! Shabbat starts on Friday evening, eighteen minutes before sunset, and ends on Saturday evening, about an hour after sunset. Shabbat is a day of rest. On Shabbat, many families do no work. Instead, many of us go to synagogue and spend time with family and friends. On Friday night, we light candles to welcome the Sabbath and say blessings over food, including the delicious braided bread called *challah*. If you want to wish someone a peaceful Sabbath, say, "Shabbat shalom."

ROSH HASHANAH literally means "Head of the Year" and is the Jewish New Year. Rosh Hashanah falls on the first two days of the Jewish month of Tishri, which can land in either September or October. On Rosh Hashanah, we go to synagogue to pray and to hear the blowing of the *shofar* (ram's horn) to welcome the new year. It is traditional to eat apples and honey to ensure a sweet year. If you want to wish someone a happy new year, say, "Shanah Tovah."

YOM KIPPUR, the Day of Atonement, occurs on the tenth day of the Jewish month of Tishri, beginning just before sunset of the ninth day of Tishri and lasting until just after sunset of the tenth day of Tishri. It is the most somber day of the year. No work is done, and many of us who are over the age of thirteen and healthy fast until the holiday is over. At synagogue, many prayers are said, including prayers that help remember loved ones who are no longer with us. At the end of the holiday, a "Break-Fast" meal is served and eaten joyfully with family and friends.

SUKKOT is a Hebrew word that means "huts." It is also the name of the Jewish festival that gives thanks for the autumn harvest. We celebrate Sukkot by building a *sukkah*, or hut, where we eat festive meals during the nine-day holiday. The roof of the sukkah is made of loosely woven twigs, so that when we stand inside the sukkah in the evening we can look up and see the stars.

SIMCHAT TORAH: Every week, Jews all over the world read the same portion of the Torah during Shabbat services. On Simchat Torah, which means "Rejoicing of the Law," the yearly cycle ends and immediately begins again. On Simchat Torah, we affirm that the Torah is "the tree of life" by taking it down from the ark and dancing it around the temple seven times with great joy.

CHANUKAH is a Hebrew word that means "dedication." It is the name of the eight-day holiday that celebrates the victory of the Macabees over the armies of Syria in 174 BCE. During that time, the Macabees rebuilt the Holy Temple of Jerusalem, but they had oil to light the *menorah* for only one night. A miracle happened: the oil burned for eight nights! To celebrate Chanukah, we light the menorah as follows: on the first night we light the *shamash* (helper candle) and one candle; then we add a candle every night for a total of eight nights. On Chanukah, we also spin the *dreidel*, eat *latkes* (potato pancakes), and give our loved ones gifts.

TU B'SHEVAT, which means "the fifteenth day of the month of Shevat," is the New Year of the Trees. To celebrate Tu B'Shevat, we plant trees, both at home and in Israel, often in honor and in memory of our loved ones. Some families prepare a special meal called a "Tu B'Shevat seder." At the seder, we say special blessings over the fruit of the trees, study, and sing.

PURIM, which means "lots," is celebrated by reading a special scroll called the *Megillah*, which tells the story of Queen Esther, who, along with her cousin Mordecai, saved the Jews from destruction by the evil king Haman. Haman drew "lots" to determine which would be the best day to destroy the Jews. But he did not succeed! During Purim we dress in costume when we go to synagogue, and when the story of Queen Esther is read out loud, we shout, boo, hiss, and make lots of noise with our *groggers* (noisemakers) each time Haman's name is mentioned!

PASSOVER (or "Pesach" in Hebrew) is an eight-day festival that celebrates the exodus of the Jews from Egypt more than three thousand years ago. The story of Passover is told at home, at a service called a *seder*, which means "order" and includes a festive meal. There are many rituals during the seder, such as the washing of the hands, the asking of the four questions, and saying specific blessings and eating certain foods, all done in a particular order. During the eight days of Passover, many of us eat only unleavened bread (*matzah*) to remind us that our ancestors had to flee Egypt in such a hurry that they couldn't even wait for their bread dough to rise.

SHAVUOT celebrates the giving of the Torah to the Jewish people. The word *shavuot* means "weeks," and the holiday falls exactly seven weeks after the second day of Passover. On Shavuot, some of us stay up all night long to study the Torah! Shavuot also celebrates the harvesting of the wheat and the ripening of the first fruit. We eat a dairy meal on Shavuot, because Israel is known as the "land of milk and honey."

HOLIDAY CRAFTS AND RECIPES

Use only nontoxic, child-friendly materials, such as paint, glue, crayons, and markers. Any sharp object, like a knife, should be handled only by an adult. Always remember to lay old newspapers or other paper on your work surface to protect it. And have fun!

NAMING CEREMONY: WELCOME HOME BANNER

You will need:

poster board or large piece of construction paper
pencil
glitter glue
crayons
markers
paint

Using the pencil, write "Welcome Home" and the new baby's name in the middle of the paper. Trace over the pencil with glitter glue. Let dry overnight. Decorate the rest of the paper by drawing pictures of your family on it with crayons, markers, or paint. Hang your banner in the baby's room so she can see how much you love her!

SHABBAT: CHALLAH COVER

You will need:

large white cloth napkin (approx. 20″ x 20″)
fabric marker
finger paint
Popsicle stick
paper plate

Using the fabric marker, write "Shabbat Shalom" or "challah" in the center of the cloth napkin. Use English and/or Hebrew letters. Then pour finger paint onto the paper plate and spread it around using the Popsicle stick. Press your hand into the finger paint and then press your hand onto the cloth napkin, leaving an imprint—but don't cover up the words you have written. Have each member of your family place a handprint on the napkin. Allow the cloth to dry. On Friday night when the challah is uncovered, all members of your family can hold the challah, pull it apart, and enjoy it together.

Hebrew letters for Shabbot Shalom: שבת שלום
Hebrew letters for Challah: חלה

ROSH HASHANA: NEW YEAR'S CARDS

You will need:

9″ x 12″ construction paper
blunt scissors
colored marker
large potato
kitchen knife
acrylic paint
paper towels
paper plate

Cut the construction paper in half so that each piece measures 6″ by 9″. Fold each half in half to make a blank card. Have an adult cut the potato in half. Draw a large triangle on the flat surface of one potato half. Have an adult use the kitchen knife to cut away the part of the potato outside the triangle to create a raised stamp. Spread some paint on the paper plate. Dip the potato half with the triangle on it into the paint and then press it onto a paper towel once or twice to remove excess paint. Then press the triangle onto the front of your card, in the middle, so that the imprint of the triangle is upside down. Then dip the triangle into the paint again, press it onto the paper towel once or twice to remove excess paint, and press it onto the same card so that the imprint is right side up and overlaps the first triangle. Ta-da! You have decorated the front of your card with a Jewish star. Let the star dry for several hours. Write "Happy New Year" or "Shanah Tovah" inside your card. Make as many as you'd like. Your friends and family will love them!

YOM KIPPUR: NOODLE KUGEL FOR THE BREAK-FAST

You will need:

1 package flat egg noodles (8 oz.)
3 eggs
¾ cup milk
¼ cup butter, softened, plus extra to grease the pan
½ cup sugar
1 tsp. cinnamon
1 tsp. vanilla
1 lb. cottage cheese
large pot with lid
colander
small bowl
large mixing bowl
measuring cup
measuring spoons
fork
8-inch square pan

Using the large pot, have an adult cook the noodles according to the directions on the package. Drain in the colander.
Preheat the oven to 350 °F. (Make sure an adult is present when using the oven.)
Butter the pan.
Crack the eggs into the small bowl and beat with the fork.
In the large mixing bowl, mix together the eggs, milk, butter, sugar, cinnamon, vanilla, and cottage cheese.
Add the noodles.
Pour the noodle mixture into the pan. Have an adult place the pan in the oven. Bake for 80 to 90 minutes. You will know the kugel is done when the top is slightly browned. It will be HOT! Let cool for about 10 minutes before serving. Enjoy!

SUKKOT: EDIBLE SUKKAH

You will need:

4 square crackers
cream cheese
pretzel sticks
paper plate
butter knife

Place one cracker on the paper plate. (This is the "floor" of your sukkah!) Spread a thick line of cream cheese around three sides of the perimeter of the cracker. Stand one cracker along one edge of the floor and push down into the cream cheese. (This is the first "wall" of your sukkah.) Spread some cream cheese on the very edge of one side of another cracker and place it next to the first wall of your sukkah at a right angle. (This is the second wall of your sukkah.) Spread some cream cheese along the very edge of one side of another cracker and place it next to the second wall of your sukkah at a right angle. (This is the third wall of your sukkah.) Leave the fourth wall open, as a doorway. Lay the pretzel sticks across the top of your sukkah to make the roof. Remember to leave spaces between the pretzels so that anyone standing inside your sukkah could look up and see the stars!

SIMCHAT TORAH: EDIBLE TORAH

You will need:

1 extra-large flat tortilla
jar of almond butter
chocolate sprinkles
2 large pretzel rods
licorice string
sharp knife
butter knife
flat cutting board

Place the tortilla on the cutting board. Have an adult use the sharp knife to cut a rectangle out of the tortilla. It should measure approximately 6″ high and 8″ wide. Using the butter knife, cover the rectangle with almond butter. Scatter chocolate sprinkles over the almond butter in rows to represent Hebrew letters. Place one pretzel rod on each end of the tortilla rectangle and roll inward, so that the tortilla wraps around each pretzel rod. When the two pretzel rods meet in the middle, tie the "Torah" together with a piece of licorice string. As you bite into the Torah, think about how delicious it is to hear it read aloud.

CHANUKAH: LATKES

You will need:

4 large potatoes
2 eggs
½ cup matzah meal
oil
grater
large bowl
small bowl
fork
measuring cup
frying pan
large spoon
spatula
paper towels
sour cream
applesauce

With an adult, peel and grate the potatoes. Put them into the large bowl and drain the excess liquid. Crack the eggs into the small bowl and beat them with the fork. Add the matzah meal and beaten eggs to the potatoes and mix well. Have an adult cover the bottom of the frying pan with about an inch of oil and heat it over a high flame. Drop dollops of the potato batter into the frying pan (2 to 3 tablespoons per dollop) and flatten with the spatula. Cook the latkes over high heat until golden brown and crispy-looking. Then flip them with the spatula and cook them until the other sides are also golden brown. Drain the latkes on paper towels and serve with applesauce and sour cream. Delicious!

TU B'SHEVAT: GROW A PARSLEY PLANT!

You will need:

1 packet parsley seeds
bowl
warm water
clay pot (at least 10″ deep) and saucer
gravel
potting soil
sunny windowsill
liquid fertilizer
patience!

Place the parsley seeds in the bowl, fill with warm water, and let them soak for 24 hours. Fill the bottom of the clay pot with ½″ of gravel and place on the saucer. Fill the rest of the pot with potting soil. Plant the seeds about ⅛″ deep. Water the soil and keep it moist (but not overly wet) at all times. It will take 3 to 4 weeks for you to see the parsley start to grow. New parsley plants will look like blades of grass. When the parsley starts to grow, place it in a very sunny spot. Parsley needs between 4 and 6 hours of direct sunlight every day. When the shoots are about 3″ long, thin them out so only two or three plants remain. Fertilize once a week. After about 14 weeks, your parsley will be ready to harvest! Snip at the bottom of the stalk with scissors. New growth will appear and your plant will continue to grow as long as you continue to care for it.

PURIM: GROGGER (NOISEMAKER)

You will need:

1 box macaroni, ziti, or other pasta
piece of brown paper large enough to wrap the box
tape
crayons
markers

Decorate your paper with symbols of Purim, such as *hammentaschen* cookies, Jewish stars, and Queen Esther's crown. Wrap the unopened box of pasta with your paper, as if you are wrapping a present. Then shake it up and down as loudly as you can whenever the evil Haman's name is mentioned! When the holiday is over, remove and recycle the paper, and donate the pasta to your local food pantry.

PASSOVER: SEDER PLATE PLACEMATS

You will need:

construction paper (one piece for each placemat,
    about 12" x 18")
large round dinner plate
small glass
marker
crayons
clear contact paper
blunt scissors

Trace around the plate on a piece of construction paper with your marker. Place the small glass in the center of the drawn circle and trace it around with the marker. Use the glass to trace five circles around the center circle. Use the crayons to write the name of, or draw, one seder plate item in each of the small circles: roasted shank bone, roasted or boiled egg, maror (bitter herbs such as horseradish), charoses (a mixture of apples, walnuts, cinnamon, and grape juice), karpas (greens such as celery, parsley, or lettuce), and salt water. Make a placemat for each family member and seder guest. You can personalize each placemat by writing the person's name on it. Cover each placemat with contact paper to protect it. Trim the edges if necessary. Each guest may now take a placemat home as a souvenir of your seder!

SHAVUOT: LAND OF MILK AND HONEY MILKSHAKE

You will need:

3 scoops vanilla ice cream
¼ teaspoon vanilla extract
½ cup milk
½ teaspoon honey
measuring cup
measuring spoons
blender
tall glass
straw

Place all of the ingredients in the blender, cover it tightly, and blend until smooth. Pour your milkshake into the glass, and sip through the straw. Easy! This makes enough for one very hungry person. It can also be shared by two friends!